Mandala Coloring Book for Kids

DREAM. INSPIRE. CREATE.

VISIT US ONLINE:
www.youngdreamerspress.com

TAG US IN YOUR PHOTOS & VIDEOS:
www.instagram.com/youngdreamerspress
www.tiktok.com/@youngdreamerspress

WE'RE ALSO ON FACEBOOK:
www.facebook.com/youngdreamerspress

BUT WAIT, THERE'S MORE!

VISIT GO.YOUNGDREAMERSPRESS.COM/MANDALAS

To join our newsletter and
make their world more colorful with
free printable coloring pages!

All pages sized for 8.5 x 11 paper and include a wide range of subjects including:
animals, kittens, mermaids, unicorns, mandalas, an astronaut, planets,
a firetruck, a construction vehicle, cupcakes, and more!

Also Available from
Young Dreamers Press

www.YoungDreamersPress.com

978-1-989790-93-9

978-1-990136-17-7

978-1-990136-39-9

978-1-990136-04-7

978-1-990136-05-4

978-1-990136-35-1

978-1-990136-57-3

978-1-990136-52-8

978-1-990136-18-4

978-1-989790-36-6

978-1-990136-09-2

978-1-990136-16-0

978-1-990136-38-2

978-1-989790-96-0

978-1-990136-02-3

978-1-989790-94-6

978-1-989790-69-4

978-1-990136-01-6

978-1-989387-13-9

978-1-989387-46-7

978-1-989387-94-8

978-1-989387-96-2

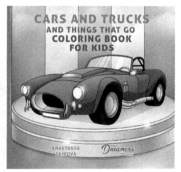

978-1-989790-09-0

978-1-989790-13-7

978-1-989790-41-0

978-1-989790-64-9

978-1-989387-87-0

978-1-989387-88-7

978-1-777375-33-1

978-1-990136-03-0

978-1-990136-07-8

978-1-989790-95-3

978-1-777375-31-7

978-1-777375-32-4

Printed in the USA
CPSIA information can be obtained
at www.ICGtesting.com
LVHW082237220124
769679LV00024B/345